BRAIN FITNESS BOOT CAMP

—TOUGH—
MIND FIELD

This is a Carlton Book

Published by Carlton Books Limited
20 Mortimer Street
London W1T 3JW

Copyright © 2012 Carlton Books Limited

ISBN 978 1 84732 937 0

The puzzles in this book were previously published in *Brain Training Puzzles Difficult Book 1*.

Printed in China

BRAIN FITNESS BOOT CAMP

—TOUGH—
MIND FIELD

CARLTON

Introduction

Welcome back to *Brain Fitness Boot Camp*.

Only the smartest, fastest minds can sign up for the tough puzzles in this book. You think you're one of the mental elite? That's good because confidence is something we expect from a would-be genius.

Are you ready to push your brain cells to the limit and enter the most intense phase of your training? You'll need superior observation, lightning logic and the ability to think laterally to survive this mental barrage. The puzzles in this book don't take prisoners.

Always remember that your brain is one of the most amazing things you'll ever possess, so look after it. As well as keeping it busy, you should try to get enough sleep, eat a balanced diet and keep your stress levels down – and there's no better antidote to stress than having some fun. Yet another good reason for using this book.

So, no matter how tough it gets, remember to have fun!

Sergeant O'Brain. Drill Instructor.
Brain Fitness Boot Camp.

Odd One Out

Which of the shapes below is not the same as the other ones?

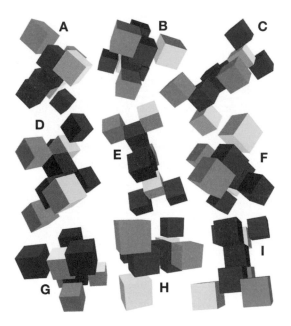

Answer on page 157

Pattern Pairs

Only one of the tiles below is unique; the others all have an exact matching pair. Can you find the one-off?

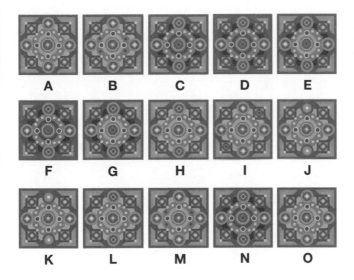

A B C D E

F G H I J

K L M N O

Answer on page 157

Minesweeper

The numbers in some squares in the grid indicate the exact number of black squares that should surround it. Shade these squares until all the numbers are surrounded by the correct number of black squares.

0			1	2			2
1		2	1				2
		2		2	2	2	
2		2					0
	1	1	2		2	1	
2		1		2		2	1
	3			3	5		3
2		2	2				

Answer on page 157

Masyu

Draw a single continuous line around the grid that passes through all the circles. The line must enter and leave each box in the centre of one of its four sides.
Black Circle: Turn left or right in the box, and the line must pass straight through the next and previous boxes.
White Circle: Travel straight through the box, and the line must turn in the next and/or previous box.

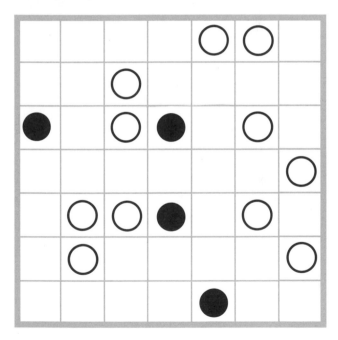

Answer on page 157

Where's the Pair?

Only two of the shapes below are exactly the same. Can you find the matching pair?

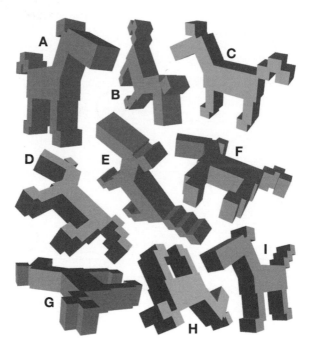

Answer on page 157

All Change

The colour of each hexagon in pattern B is directly related to the colours in pattern A. Can you apply the same rules and fill in pattern C?

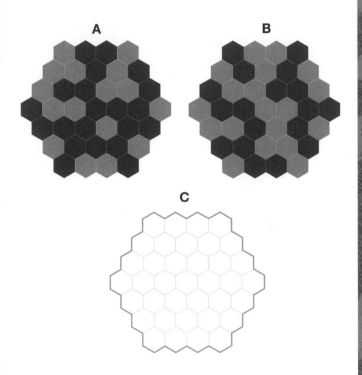

A

B

C

Answer on page 157

Camp Conifer

Every tree ▲ has one tent ▲ found horizontally or vertically adjacent to it. No tent can be in an adjacent square to another tent (even diagonally). The numbers by each row and column tell you how many tents are there. Can you locate all the tents?

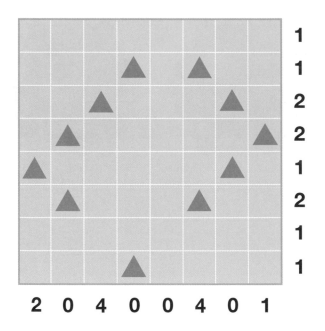

Answer on page 157

Codoku Six

Complete the first grid so that every row and column contains all the letters BCIMU and W. Do the same with grid 2 and the numbers 12345 and 6. To decode the finished grids, add the numbers in the shaded squares to the letters in the matching squares in the first grid (ie: A + 3 = D, Y + 4 = C) to get six new letters which can be arranged to spell the name of a city.

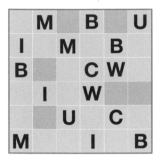

Answer on page 157

Cube Volume

These little cubes originally made a big cube measuring 20 cm × 20 cm × 20 cm. Now that some of the little cubes have been removed, can you work out the volume of the remaining cubes? Assume all invisible cubes are present.

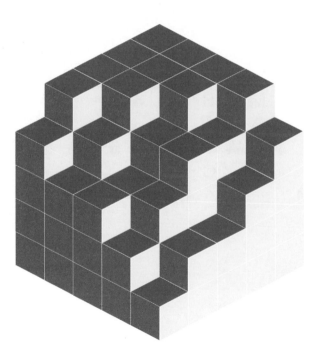

Answer on page 158

The Great Divide

Divide up the grid into four equal sized, equally shaped parts, each containing four circles of four different colours.

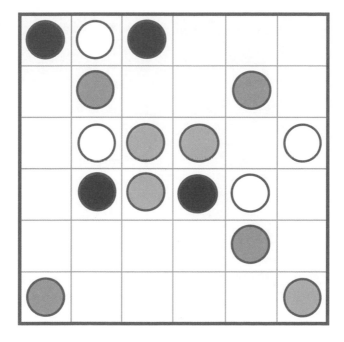

Answer on page 158

Where's the Pair?

Only two of these pictures are exactly the same. Can you spot the matching pair?

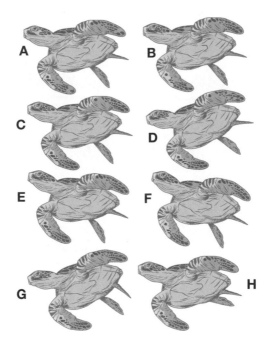

Answer on page 158

Sudoku

Complete the grid so that all rows and columns, and each outlined block of nine squares, contain the numbers 1, 2, 3, 4, 5, 6, 7, 8 and 9.

		3		7				
6	5			9			3	
7			5		8	2	1	
	6			2	1		4	
3			4					
	9				5			
5	1					8		7
						1		
2		8		7		5	6	4

Answer on page 158

Scene It?

The four squares below can all be found in the picture grid — can you track them down? Beware, they may not be the right way up!

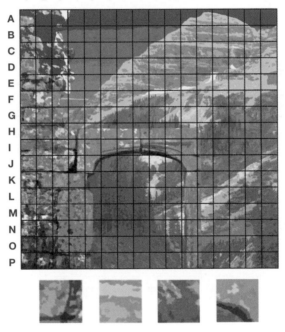

Answer on page 158

18

Think Back

Study these images for a minute, then cover them up and answer the five questions below.

Questions:
1. How many places in front of the green car is the red car?
2. What number car is second?
3. What is the total of the numbers on the first two cars?
4. What number car is in front of the yellow one?
5. What colour car is directly behind car number 1?

Answer on page 158

Pattern Pairs

Only one of the tiles below is unique; the others all have an exact matching pair. Can you find the one-off?

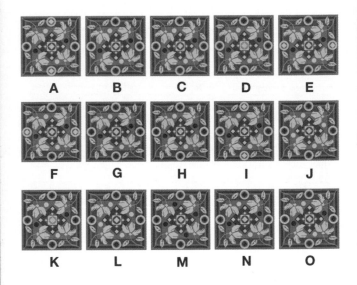

A   B   C   D   E

F   G   H   I   J

K   L   M   N   O

Answer on page 158

Percentage Point

Can you determine what percentage of this honeycomb is occupied by bees, and what percentage of the bees are awake?

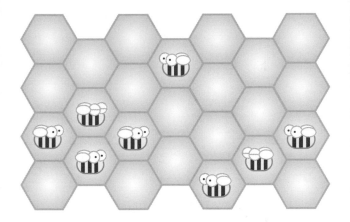

Answer on page 158

Minesweeper

The numbers in some squares in the grid indicate the exact number of black squares that should surround it. Shade these squares until all the numbers are surrounded by the correct number of black squares.

	2	2		2	3		3
2			3				
	3	3		2	3		3
3			3	3		2	2
	3	4			1	2	
1				3			
2	4	4	3		2		
			1	1		2	1

Answer on page 159

Logic Sequence

The balls below have been rearranged. Can you work out the new sequence of the balls from the clues given below?

The square is immediately to the right of the X.
The circle is between the X and the triangle.
There are two balls between the circle and the star.

Answer on page 159

A Piece of Pie

Can you crack the pie code and work out what number belongs where the question mark is?

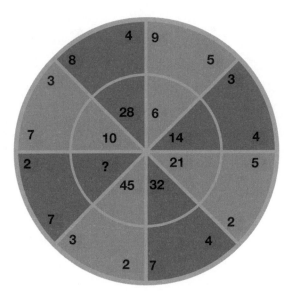

Answer on page 159

All Change

The colour of each triangle in pattern B is directly related to the colours in pattern A. Can you apply the same rules and fill in pattern C?

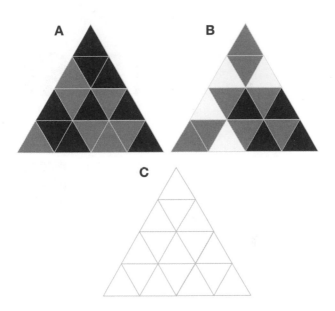

A

B

C

Answer on page 159

Dice Maze

The colours on these dice represent a direction – up, down, left and right. Starting in the middle die of the grid, follow the instructions correctly and you will visit every die in turn once only. What's the last die you visit on your trip?

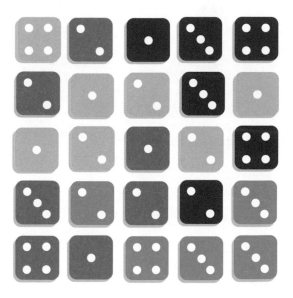

Answer on page 159

Five-Point Problem

Discover the pattern behind the numbers on these pentagons and fill in the blanks to complete the puzzle.

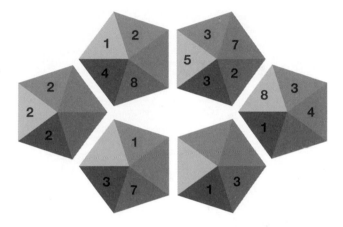

Answer on page 159

The Great Divide

Divide up the grid into four equal sized, equally shaped parts, each containing one of all four symbols.

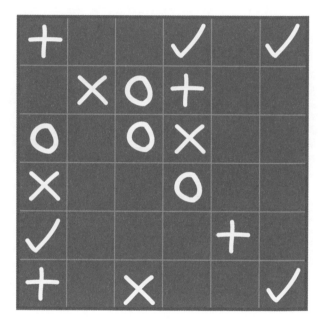

Answer on page 159

Killer Six

Complete the grid so that all rows and columns contain the numbers 1, 2, 3, 4, 5 and 6. Areas with a dotted outline contain numbers that add up to the total shown.

11	16			3	10
	4		4		
13	5			11	
		6	**4**		11
3			7		
	11			7	

Answer on page 159

Knight's Move

Find an empty square in the grid that is one chess knight's move away from a blue, red and yellow circle. A knight's move is an 'L' shape — two squares sideways, up or down in any direction, followed by one square to the left or right.

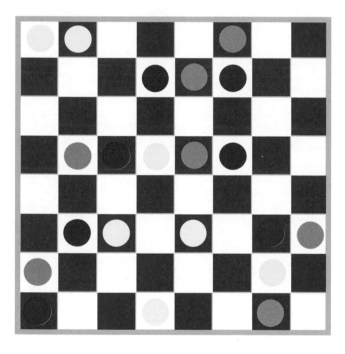

Answer on page 160

Looplink

Connect adjacent dots with either horizontal or vertical lines to create a continuous unbroken loop which never crosses over itself. Some, but not all of the boxes are numbered. The numbers in these boxes tell you how many sides of that box are used by your unbroken line.

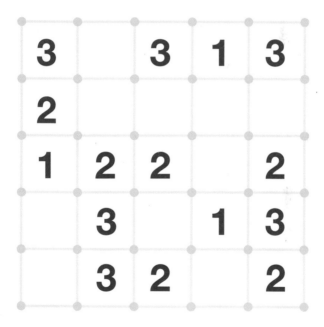

Answer on page 160

Masyu

Draw a single continuous line around the grid that passes through all the circles. The line must enter and leave each box in the centre of one of its four sides.

Black Circle: Turn left or right in the box, and the line must pass straight through the next and previous boxes.

White Circle: Travel straight through the box, and the line must turn in the next and/or previous box.

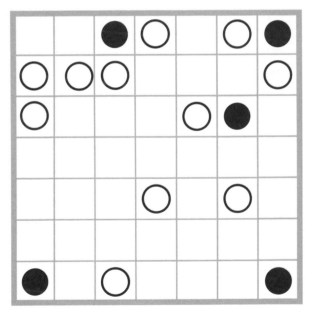

Answer on page 160

Mini Nonogram

The numbers by each row and column describe black squares and groups of black squares that are adjoining. Colour in all the black squares and a six number combination will be revealed.

					1									
					1									
					1									
				5	1	5			5				1	
				5	1	5		3	1	5		1	5	5
	3	1	3											
1	1	1	1											
	3	1	1											
1	1	1	1											
	3	1	1											
3	1	1	1											
1	1	1	1	1										
	1	1	3	1										
	1	1	1	1										
		3	1	1										

Answer on page 160

Mirror Image

Only one of these pictures is an exact mirror image of the first one. Can you spot it?

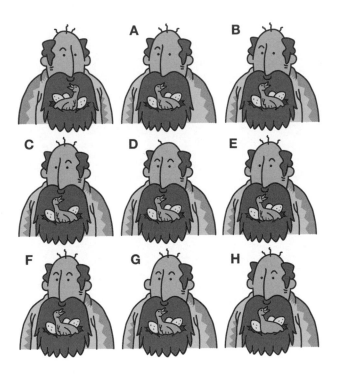

Answer on page 160

More or Less

The arrows indicate whether a number in a box is greater or smaller than an adjacent number. Complete the grid so that all rows and columns contain the numbers 1 to 5.

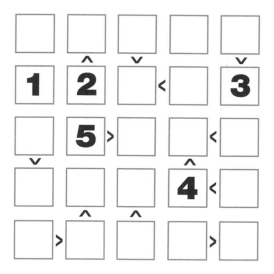

Answer on page 160

Odd One Out

Which of the shapes below is not the same as the other ones?

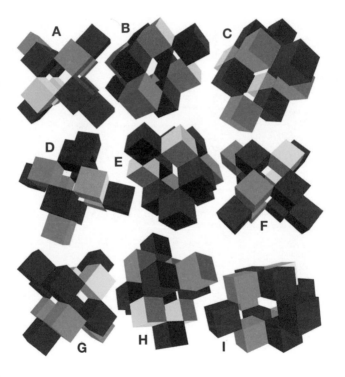

Answer on page 160

Pattern Pairs

Ony one of the tiles below is unique; the others all have an exact matching pair. Can you find the one-off?

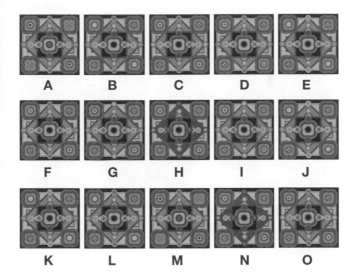

A B C D E

F G H I J

K L M N O

Answer on page 160

Plan View

Three of the patterns are a flat view of the picture below. Can you find the three that do not match?

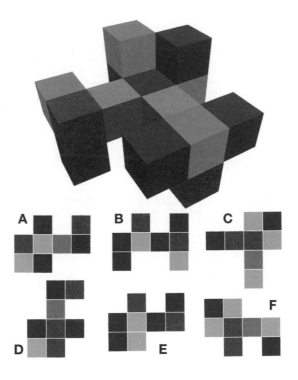

A   B   C

D   E   F

Answer on page 161

Scene It?

The four squares below can all be found in the picture grid – can you track them down? Beware, they may not be the right way up!

Answer on page 161

Shape Stacker

Can you work out the logic behind the numbers in these shapes, and the total of A x B x C?

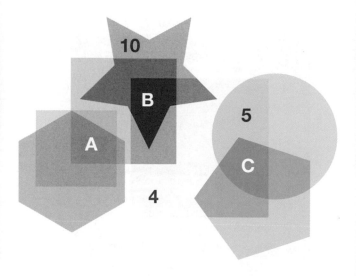

Answer on page 161

Silhouette

Which of the coloured-in pics matches our silhouette?

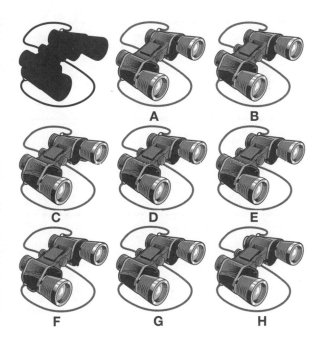

A

B

C

D

E

F

G

H

Answer on page 161

Sudoku

Complete the grid so that all rows and columns, and each outlined block of nine squares, contain the numbers 1, 2, 3, 4, 5, 6, 7, 8 and 9.

	1				3	5		4
	3	6					9	8
		2		7	1			6
		2				9		
3	4						8	
		8	3			2		5
		1	6		8			
5	9	7					6	
			2				7	1

Answer on page 161

Sum People

Work out what number is represented by which person and replace the question mark.

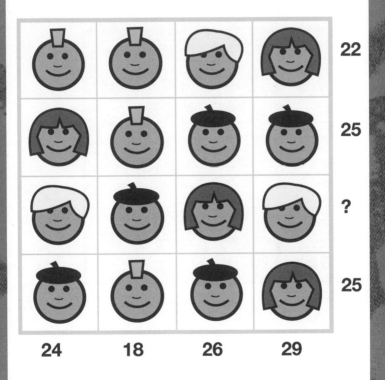

Answer on page 161

Sum People

Work out what number is represented by which person and replace the question mark.

Weigh to Go

The coloured balls represent the numbers 2, 3, 4, 5 and 6. Can you work out which is which, and therefore how many green balls are required to balance the final scale?

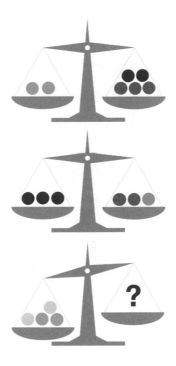

Answer on page 161

Where's the Pair?

Only two of the shapes below are exactly the same — can you find the matching pair?

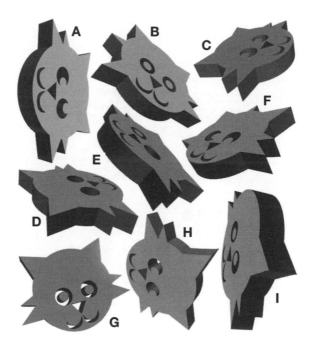

Answer on page 162

Same Difference

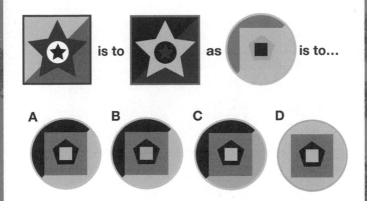

is to ... as ... is to...

A   B   C   D

Answer on page 162

Scene It?

The four squares below can all be found in the picture grid — can you track down? Beware, they may not be the right way up!

Answer on page 162

Mirror Image

Only one of these pictures is an exact mirror image of the first one.
Can you spot it?

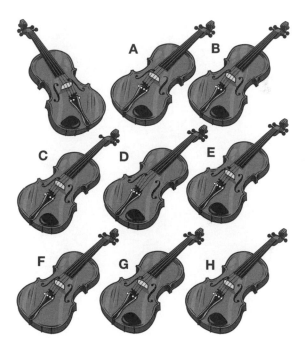

Answer on page 162

View from Above

Of the plan views below, only one of them is a true overhead representation of the scene shown here – can you work out which?

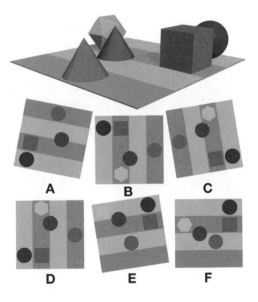

Answer on page 162

Can You Cut It?

Cut two straight lines through this shape to create three shapes that are identical.

Answer on page 162

Dice Maze

The colours on these dice represent a direction — up, down, left and right. Starting in the middle dice of the grid, follow the instructions correctly and you will visit every die in turn once only. What's the last die you visit on your trip?

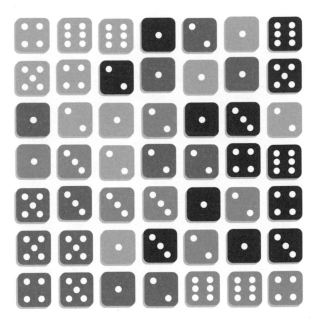

Answer on page 162

Dice Puzzle

Which of these dice is not like the other three?

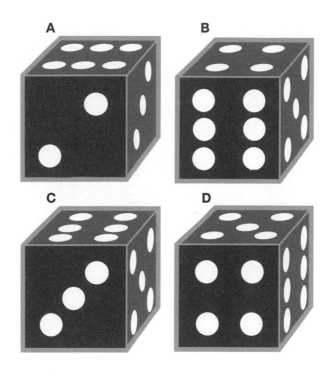

A

B

C

D

Answer on page 162

Floor Fillers

Below is a plan of a bathroom, showing the bath and other fixings, and next to it, some very oddly shaped pieces of marble. Can you arrange them to fill the floor?

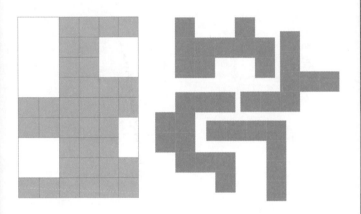

Answer on page 163

Hub Signs

What number should appear in the hub of the second wheel?

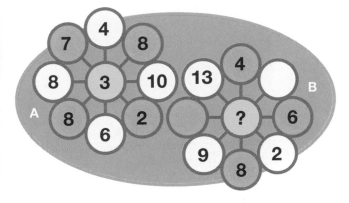

Answer on page 163

Jigsaw

Which four of the pieces below can complete the jigsaw and make a perfect square?

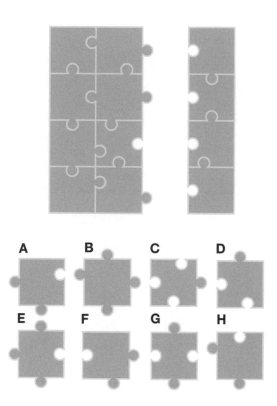

Answer on page 163

Latin Square

Complete the grid so that every row and column, and every outlined area, contains the letters A, B, C, D, E and F.

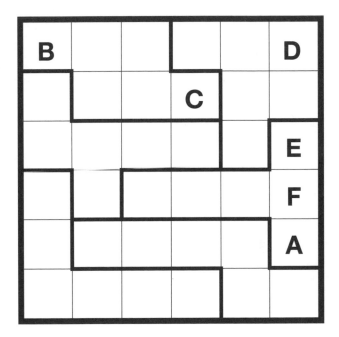

Answer on page 163

Logic Sequence

The balls below have been rearranged. Can you work out the new sequence of the balls from the clues given below?

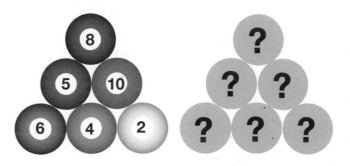

The top three balls total 22.
The 5 ball is immediately to the right of the 6, and isn't in contact with the 4 ball.
The 10 ball touches four others, but not the 6.

Answer on page 163

Minesweeper

The numbers in some squares in the grid indicate the exact number of black squares that should surround it. Shade these squares until all the numbers are surrounded by the correct number of black squares.

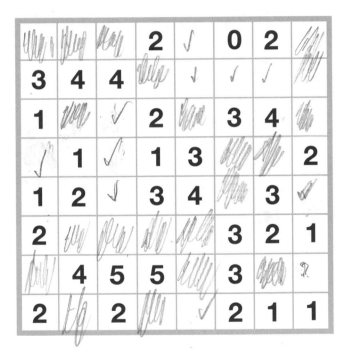

Answer on page 163

Pattern Pairs

Only one of the tiles below is unique; the other 14 all have an exact matching pair. Can you find the one-off?

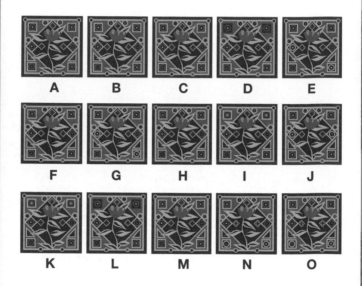

A   B   C   D   E

F   G   H   I   J

K   L   M   N   O

Answer on page 163

Shape Stacker

Can you work out the logic behind the numbers in these shapes, and the total of A + B?

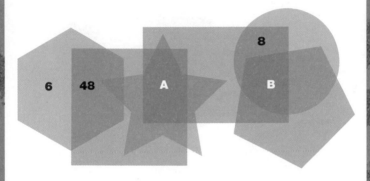

Answer on page 163

View from Above

Of the plan views below, only one of them is a true overhead representation of the scene shown here – can you work out which?

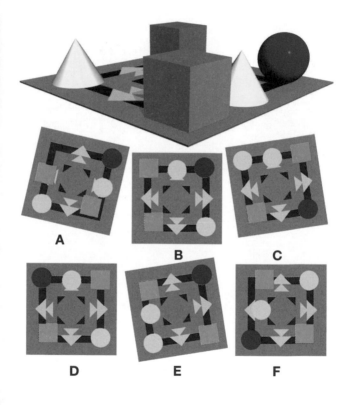

A

B

C

D

E

F

Answer on page 164

Battleships

The numbers on the side and bottom of the grid indicate occupied squares or groups of consecutive occupied squares in each row or column. Can you finish the grid so that it contains three Cruisers, three Launches and three Buoys and the numbers tally?

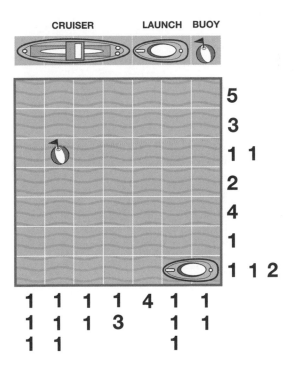

Answer on page 164

Camp Conifer

Every tree 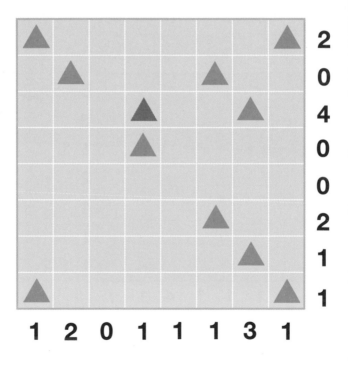 has one tent ▲ found horizontally or vertically adjacent to it. No tent can be in an adjacent square to another tent (even diagonally). The numbers by each row and column tell you how many tents are there. Can you locate all the tents?

Answer on page 164

Patch of the Day

Place the shape over the grid so that no colour appears twice in the same row or column. Beware, the shape may not be the right way up!

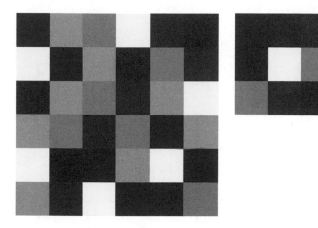

Answer on page 164

Looplink

Connect adjacent dots with either horizontal or vertical lines to create a continuous unbroken loop which never crosses over itself. Some, but not all of the boxes are numbered. The numbers in these boxes tell you how many sides of that box are used by your unbroken line.

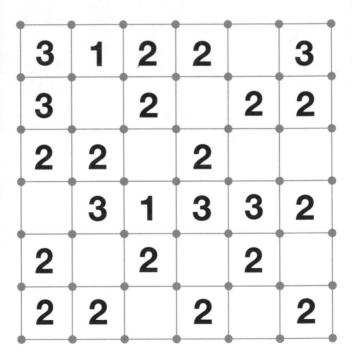

Answer on page 164

More or Less

The arrows indicate whether a number in a box is greater or smaller than an adjacent number. Complete the grid so that all rows and columns contain the numbers 1 to 6.

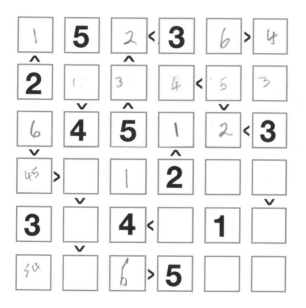

Answer on page 164

Number Chunks

Divide up the grid into four equal size, equally shaped parts, each containing numbers that add up to 40.

8	2	1	2	2	4
6	3	1	1	6	3
4	9	9	9	3	5
5	7	1	5	5	5
2	7	3	1	6	4
9	7	3	2	3	7

Answer on page 164

Safecracker

To open the safe, all the buttons must be pressed in the correct order before the "open" button is pressed. What is the first button pressed in your sequence?

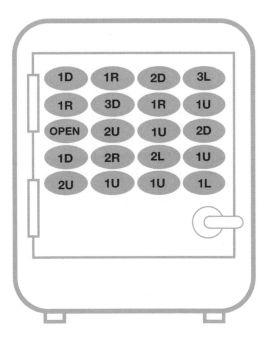

1D	1R	2D	3L
1R	3D	1R	1U
OPEN	2U	1U	2D
1D	2R	2L	1U
2U	1U	1U	1L

Answer on page 164

Sudoku

Complete the grid so that all rows and columns, and each outlined block of nine squares, contain the numbers 1, 2, 3, 4, 5, 6, 7, 8 and 9.

	2		1		8	3		
		7		2				5
4			7			1		
		1	4					8
	9					5		6
2			6	7				
7		6	8					3
8				9			2	
			3				6	4

Answer on page 165

Symbol Sums

These symbols represent the numbers 1 to 4. If the pink parrot represents the number 2, can you work out what the other parrots are representing and make a working sum?

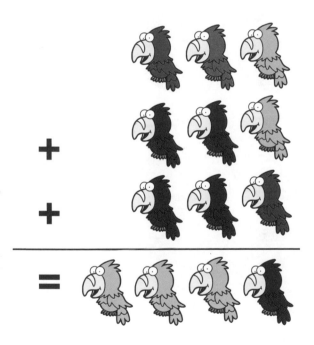

Answer on page 165

Where's the Pair?

Only two of these pictures are exactly the same. Can you spot the matching pair?

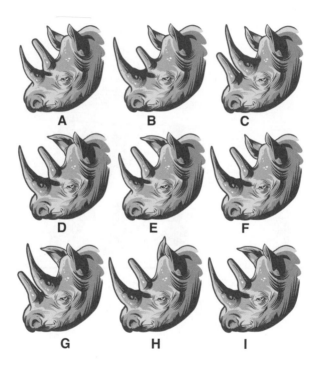

Answer on page 165

All Change

The colour of each square in pattern B is directly related to the colours in pattern A. The colours in pattern C relate to pattern B the same way. Can you apply the same rules and fill in pattern D?

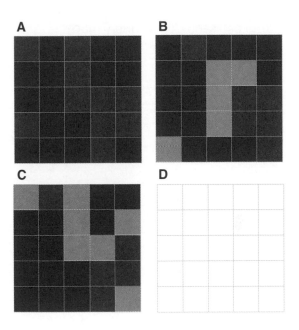

A

B

C

D

Answer on page 165

Battleships

The numbers on the side and bottom of the grid indicate occupied squares or groups of consecutive occupied squares in each row or column. Can you finish the grid so that it contains three Cruisers, four Launches and five Buoys and the numbers tally?

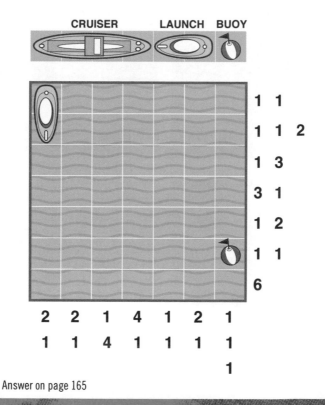

Camp Conifer

Every tree 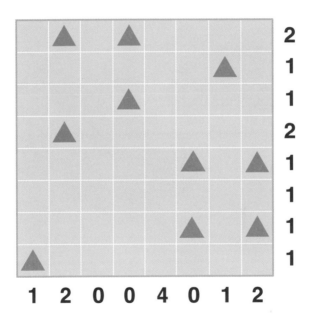 has one tent found horizontally or vertically adjacent to it. No tent can be in an adjacent square to another tent (even diagonally). The numbers by each row and column tell you how many tents are there. Can you locate all the tents?

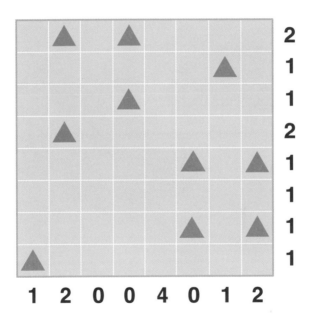

Answer on page 165

Can You Cut It?

Cut two straight lines through this shape to create three shapes that are identical.

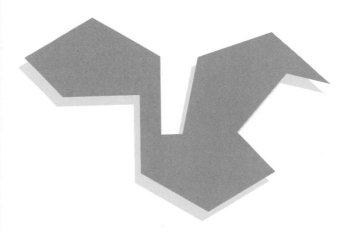

Answer on page 165

Chess

Can you place a queen, a bishop, a knight and a rook on this chessboard so that the red squares are attacked by exactly two pieces, the green one by 3 pieces and the yellow one by 4 pieces?

Answer on page 165

Five Point Problem

Discover the pattern behind the numbers on these pentagons and fill in the blanks to complete the puzzle.

Answer on page 166

Gridlock

Which square correctly completes the grid?

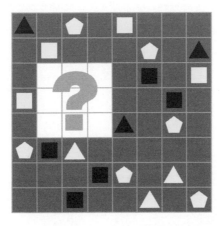

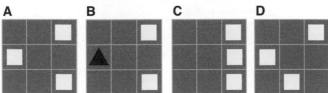

Answer on page 166

Killer Six

Complete the grid so that all rows and columns contain the numbers 1, 2, 3, 4, 5 and 6. Areas with a dotted outline contain numbers that add up to the total shown. Dotted boxes can contain the same number more than once, however.

Answer on page 166

Hub Signs

What number should appear in the hub of the second wheel?

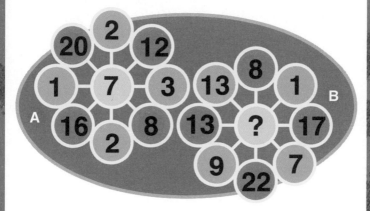

Answer on page 166

Looplink

Connect adjacent dots with either horizontal or vertical lines to create a continuous unbroken loop which never crosses over itself. Some, but not all of the boxes are numbered. The numbers in these boxes tell you how many sides of that box are used by your unbroken line.

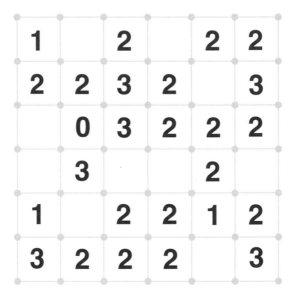

Answer on page 166

Magic Squares

Complete the square using nine consecutive numbers, so that all rows, columns and large diagonals add up to the same total.

Answer on page 166

The Great Divide

Divide up the grid into four equal size, equally shaped parts, each containing one of all four symbols.

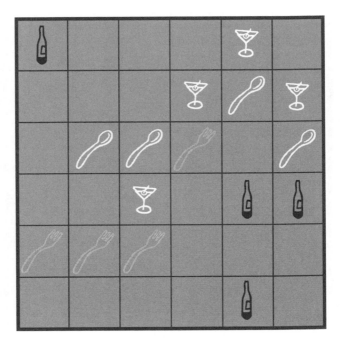

Answer on page 166

Percentage Point

Can you determine what percentage of this design is red? And what percentage of the blue squares in the design contain stars?

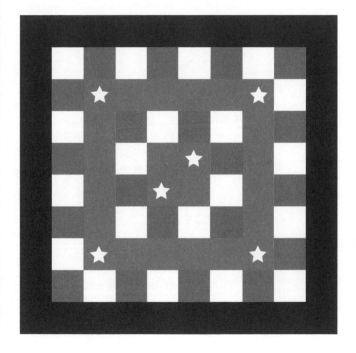

Answer on page 166

Scene It?

The four squares below can all be found in the picture grid – can you track them down? Beware, they may not be the right way up!

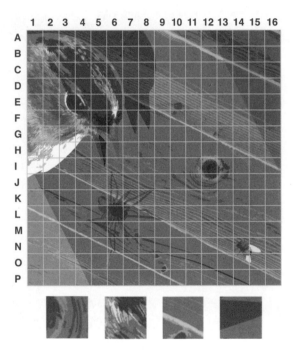

Answer on page 167

Small Logic

	Forest	Roadside	Field	Jar	Bottle	Matchbox	Morning	Afternoon	Evening
Beetle	✗	✓	✗	✓	✓	✗	✓	✗	✗
Spider	✗	✗	✓	✗	✓	✗	✗	✗	✓
Butterfly	✓	✗	✗	✗	✗	✓	✗	✓	✗
Morning	✗	✓	✓	✓	✗	✗			
Afternoon	✓	✗	✗	✗	✗				
Evening	✗	✗	✓	✗	✓	✗			
Jar	✗	✓	✓						
Bottle	✗	✗	✓						
Matchbox	✓	✗	✗						

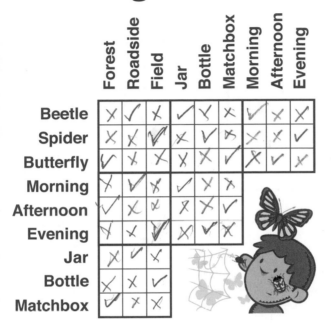

Little Tom collects insects. Can you discover where he found these three, at what time of day, and what he put them in so he could take them home?

1) The spider was found in the evening, not in a field.
2) The butterfly was found in the forest, though not in the morning, and Tom didn't put it in a jar.
3) The creature found in a field was placed in a bottle.

Answer on page 167

Sudoku

Complete the grid so that all rows and columns, and each outlined block of
nine squares, contain the numbers 1, 2, 3, 4, 5, 6, 7, 8 and 9.

		6		7		5	3	
8			1	3		2		
					2			
9				5			4	
		4			6		8	5
2	8		7	9		6		
	1			6				9
	7					4	2	1
5			4				6	

Answer on page 167

88

Think Back

Study these images for a minute, then cover them up and answer the five questions below.

Questions:
1. How many leaves has the yellow flower?
2. How many leaves in total have the flowers in red pots?
3. What colour is flower B?
4. Which flower has only the left leaf?
5. How many of the pink flowers have blue pots?

Answer on page 167

Sudoku

Fill in the numbers 1, 2, 3, 4, 5, 6, 7, 8, and 9 so they appear once only in each row, column and 9x9 grid

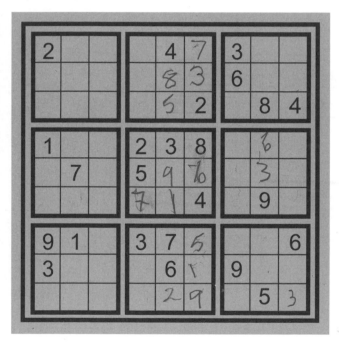

Answer on page 167

The Red Corner

Use the red corners to make the central number the same way in all three cases. What number should replace the question mark?

Answer on page 167

Chess

Can you place a queen, a bishop, a knight and a rook on this chessboard so that the red squares are attacked by exactly two pieces, the green ones by 3 pieces and the yellow one by 4 pieces?

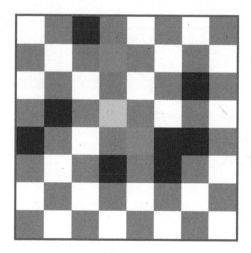

Answer on page 167

Sudoku Six

Complete the first grid so that every row and column contain all
the letters ABJKY and Z. Do the same with grid 2 and the numbers 12345 and
6. To decode the finished grid, add the numbers in the shaded squares to the
letters in the matching squares in the first grid (ie: A + 3 = D, Y + 4 = C)
to get six new letters which can be arranged to spell the name of a famous
composer.

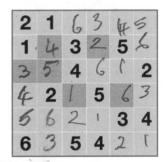

ELNDAH

HANDEL

Cube Route

Can you crack the colour code and make your way from one green square to the other? Each colour represents up, down, left or right. The blue arrow tells you which way is up...

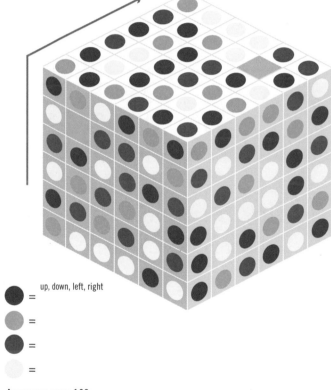

up, down, left, right

=

=

=

=

Answer on page 168

Pattern Pairs

Only one of the tiles below is unique; the others all have an exact matching pair. Can you find the one-off?

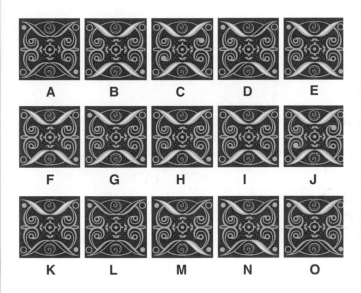

Answer on page 168

Plan View

Three of the patterns are a flat view of the picture below. Can you find the three that do not match?

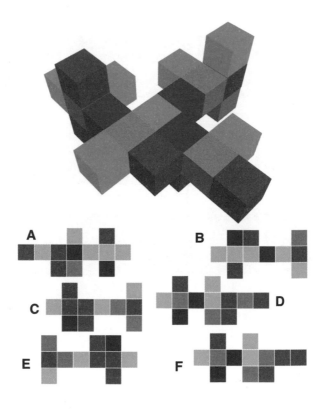

A

B

C

D

E

F

Answer on page 168

Number Mountain

Replace the question marks with numbers so that each pair of blocks adds up to the block directly above them.

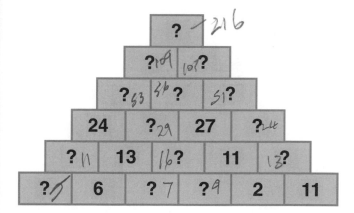

```
              ?  216

          ? 109   108 ?

       ? 55   56 ?    51 ?

    24     ? 29    27     ? 24

  ? 11   13   16 ?    11   13 ?

? 6    6    ? 7   ? 9    2    11
```

Answer on page 168

Symmetry

This picture, when finished, is symmetrical along a vertical line up the middle. Can you colour in the missing squares and work out what the picture is of?

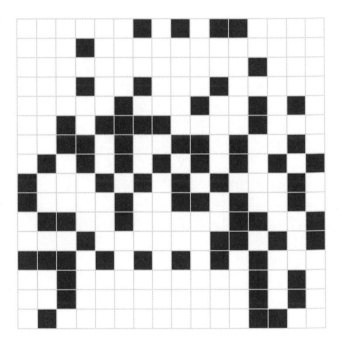

Answer on page 168

Scene It?

The four squares below can all be found in the picture grid — can you track them down? Beware, they may not be the right way up!

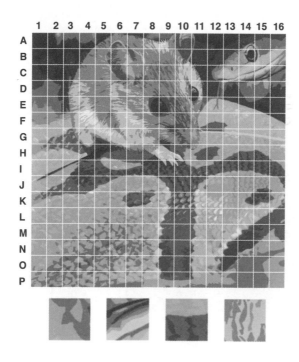

Answer on page 168

Cube Volume

These little cubes originally made a big cube measuring 15 cm x 15 cm x 15 cm. Now that some of the little cubes have been removed, can you work out the volume of the remaining cubes? Assume all invisible cubes are present.

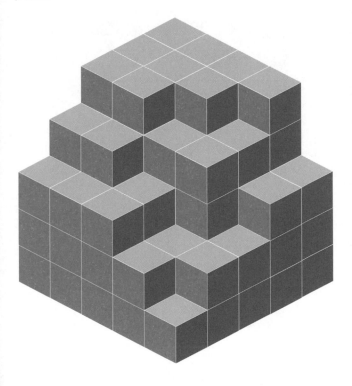

Answer on page 168

Dice Puzzle

Which of these dice is not like the other three?

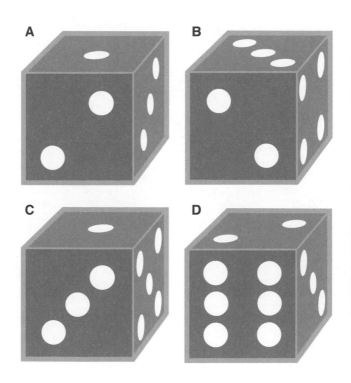

A

B

C

D

Answer on page 168

Five Star

Believe it or not, none of these stars is exactly alike. They represent every single combination of five colours - except one. Can you work out the colour placements on the missing star?

Answer on page 169

Killer Six

Complete the grid so that all rows and columns contain the numbers 1, 2, 3, 4, 5 and 6. Areas with a dotted outline contain numbers that add up to the total shown.

15	4	11		5	
			11		6
	7		**1**	6	
6	**6**	9			11
	9		9	**4**	
				6	

Answer on page 169

Masyu

Draw a single continuous line around the grid that passes through all the circles. The line must enter and leave each box in the centre of one of its four sides.

Black Circle: Turn left or right in the box, and the line must pass straight through the next and previous boxes. White Circle: Travel straight through the box, and the line must turn in the next and/or previous box.

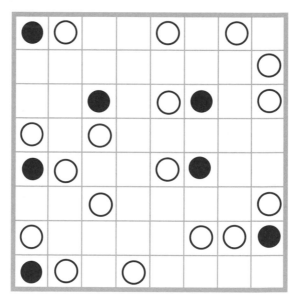

Answer on page 169

Mini Nonogram

The numbers by each row and column describe black squares and groups of black squares that are adjoining. Colour in all the black squares and a six number combination will be revealed.

							1				
		1			3	1	5			5	
	3	5	5		5	1	5		1	1	5
1 1 1 1 1											
1 1 1 1 1											
3 3 1											
1 1 1											
1 1 1											
1 3 3											
1 1 1 1											
1 1 1 1											
1 1 1 1											
1 3 1											

Answer on page 169

Number Chunks

Divide up the grid into four equal size, equally shaped parts, each containing numbers that add up to 36.

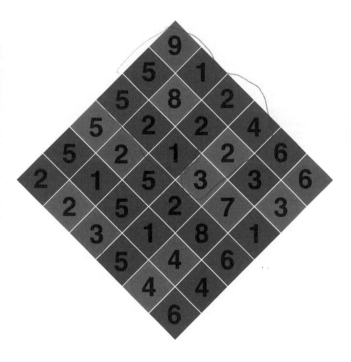

Answer on page 169

Floor Fillers

Below is a marked out floor waiting to be tiled, together with some pre-assembled groups of tiles... Can you fit them together so that they fill he floor?

Answer on page 169

Follow That

The sequence below follows a logical pattern. Can you work out which way the next pig in line faces, and what colour its tail is?

?

Answer on page 169

Jigsaw

Which four of the pieces below can complete the jigsaw and make a perfect square?

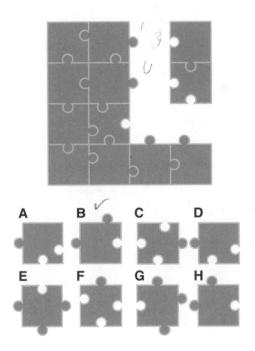

A **B** ✓ **C** **D**

E **F** **G** **H**

Answer on page 169

Logic Sequence

The balls below have been rearranged. Can you work out the new sequence of the balls from the clues given below?

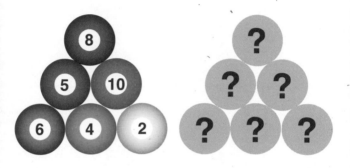

The 2 ball isn't touching the 5 or the 4.
The 4 ball is touching the 10 but not the 6.
The 8 ball is immediately to the left of the 6.
The bottom row totals 16.

Answer on page 170

Scales

The arms of these scales are divided into sections - a weight two sections away from the middle will be twice as heavy as a weight one section away. Can you arrange the supplied weights in such a way as to balance the whole scale?

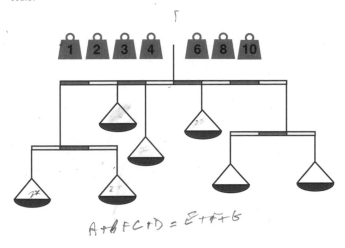

$$A + B \vdash C + D = E + F + G$$

Answer on page 170

Number Mountain

Replace the question marks with numbers so that each pair of blocks adds up to the block directly above them.

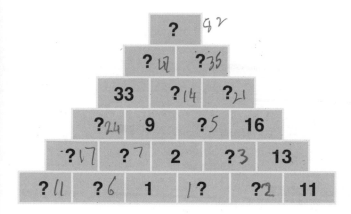

```
                    ?  42
               ? 42      ? 35
           33      ? 14      ? 21
       ? 24     9      ? 5      16
    ? 17     ? 7     2      ? 3     13
  ? 11    ? 6    1     1 ?     ? 2    11
```

Answer on page 170

Knight's Move

Find an empty square in the grid that is one chess knight's move away from a blue, red and yellow circle. A knight's move is an 'L' shape – two squares sideways, up or down in any direction, followed by one square to the left or right.

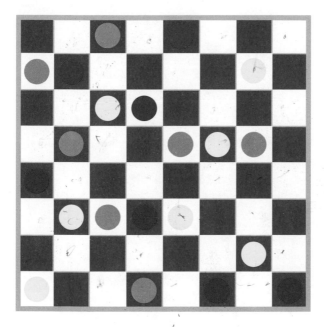

Answer on page 170

Weigh to Go

The coloured balls represent the numbers 3, 4, 5, 6 and 7. Can you work out which is which, and therefore how many red balls (unseen so far) are required to balance the final scale?

Answer on page 170

Mirror Image

Only one of these pictures is an exact mirror image of the first one.
Can you spot it?

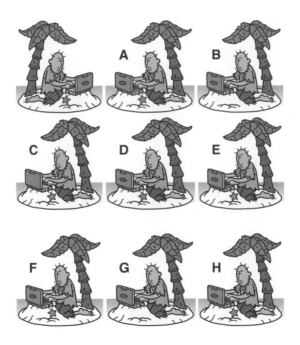

Answer on page 170

Silhouette

Which of the coloured-in pics matches our silhouette?

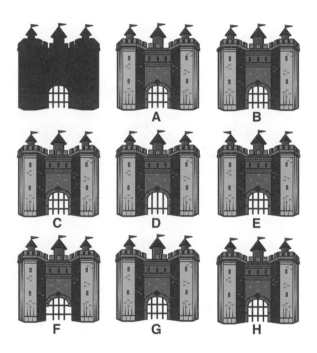

A

B

C

D

E

F

G

H

Answer on page 170

Symbol Sums

These symbols represent the numbers 1 to 4. Can you work out which colour knights are representing what numbers and make a working sum?

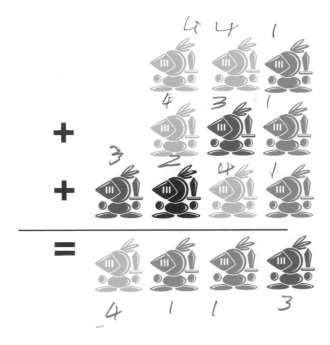

Answer on page 170

Looplink

Connect adjacent dots with either horizontal or vertical lines to create a continuous unbroken loop which never crosses over itself. Some, but not all of the boxes are numbered. The numbers in these boxes tell you how many sides of that box are used by your unbroken line.

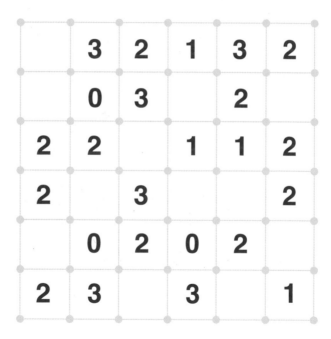

Answer on page 171

Sudoku

Complete the grid so that all rows and columns, and each outlined block of nine squares, contain the numbers 1, 2, 3, 4, 5, 6, 7, 8 and 9.

9	8	1	2	3	7	5	6	4
3	7	5	4	6	1	2	9	8
2	4	6	9	8	5	7	3	1
8	6	7	1	2	9	3	4	5
1	9	4	3	5	6	8	2	7
5	3	2	7	4	8	9	1	6
6	1	3	6	7	2	4	8	9
7	2	8	5	9	4	1	5	3
4	5	9	8	1	3	6	7	2

Answer on page 171

Matrix

Which of the four boxed figures completes the set?

Answer on page 171

Where's the Pair?

Only two of these pictures are exactly the same. Can you spot the matching pair?

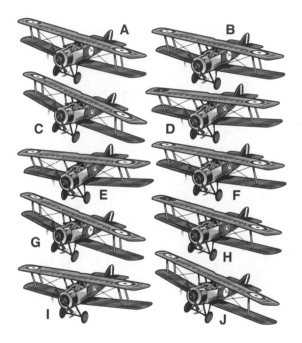

Answer on page 171

Gridlock

Which square correctly completes the grid?

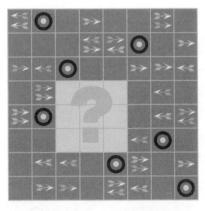

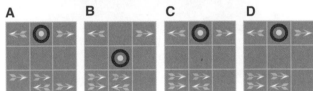

Answer on page 171

Think of a Number

Yellowbeard the pirate had 27 crew under him on his ship, the Blue Goose. He had less prisoners than that in the hold. One night, half of them escaped, leaving the ship exactly 15 percent less occupied than it was before. How many prisoners escaped?

Answer on page 171

Killer Sudoku

Complete the grid so that all rows and columns, and each outlined block of nine squares, contain the numbers 1, 2, 3, 4, 5, 6, 7, 8 and 9. Areas with a dotted outline contain numbers that add up to the total shown.

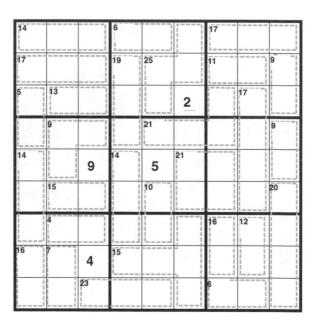

Answer on page 171

Think Back

Study these images for a minute, then cover them up and answer the five questions below.

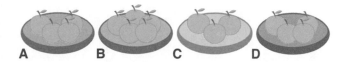

Question:
1. Which colour bowl contains only apples with leaves?
2. Which colour bowl has five apples?
3. How many apples has the bowl with three leaves?
4. How many apples have bowls A and C together?
5. How many apples in total are leafless?

Answer on page 171

Hub Signs

What number should appear in the hub of the second wheel?

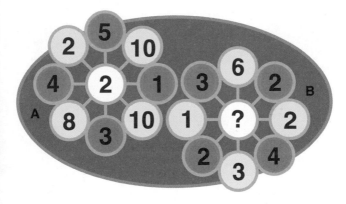

Answer on page 172

Small Logic

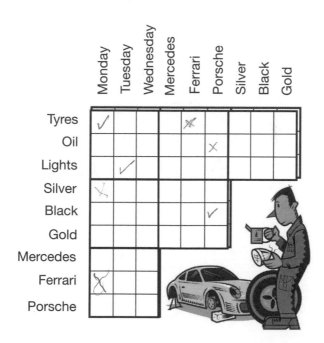

	Monday	Tuesday	Wednesday	Mercedes	Ferrari	Porsche	Silver	Black	Gold
Tyres	✓				✗				
Oil						✗			
Lights		✓							
Silver	✗								
Black						✓			
Gold									
Mercedes									
Ferrari	✗								
Porsche									

Jack's garage has seen some fancy cars this week. From the clues below, can you work out when he worked on each car, what colour each was, and what jobs he had to do?

1) The Porsche was black, and didn't need an oil change
2) Jack changed tyres on Monday, but not on the Ferrari
3) The Ferrari was done before the lights but after the silver car

Answer on page 172

In the Area

Can you work out the approximate area that this tree is occupying, minus the oranges?

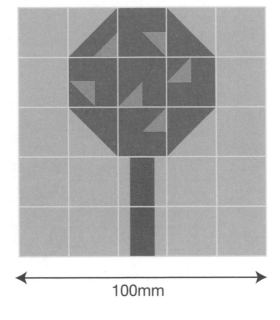

100mm

Answer on page 172

Symmetry

This picture, when finished, is symmetrical along a vertical line up the middle. Can you shade in the missing squares and work out what the picture is of?

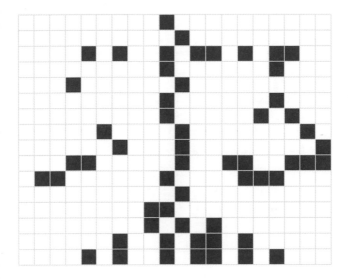

Answer on page 172

Latin Square

Complete the grid so that every row and column, and every outlined area, contains the letters A, B, C, D, E and F.

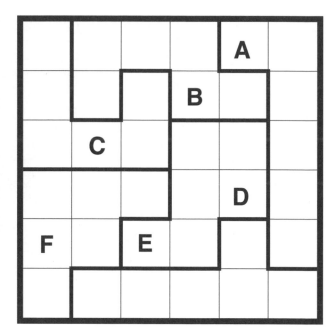

Answer on page 172

Percentage Point

Can you determine what percentage of the squares making up this design are not white, and do not contain any stars?

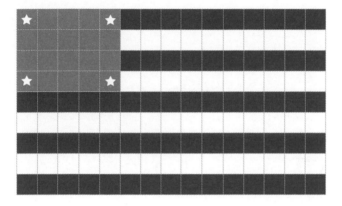

Answer on page 172

Magic Squares

Complete the square using nine consecutive numbers, so that all rows, columns and large diagonals add up to the same total.

A	B	C **14**
D	E **11**	F
G **8**	H	I

$$A + B = 19 \quad B + H = 22$$
$$F + C = 19 \quad A + D = 25$$
$$I + H = 25 \quad F + D = 22$$
$$A + F = 22$$

Answer on page 172

Revolutions

Cog A has 8 teeth, cog B has 9, cog C has 10 and cog D has 18. How many revolutions must cog A turn through to get all the cogs into an upright position?

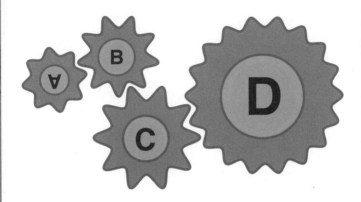

Answer on page 172

Treasure Island

The numbers on the side and bottom of the grid indicate occupied squares or groups of consecutive occupied squares in each row or column. Can you finish the grid so that it contains three of each item and the numbers tally?

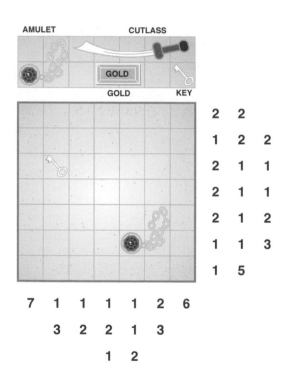

AMULET   CUTLASS

GOLD

GOLD   KEY

						2	2	
						1	2	2
						2	1	1
						2	1	1
						2	1	2
						1	1	3
						1	5	

7	1	1	1	1	2	6
3	2	2	1	3		
1	2					

Answer on page 173

Masyu

Draw a single continuous line around the grid that passes through all the circles. The line must enter and leave each box in the centre of one of its four sides.
Black Circle: Turn left or right in the box, and the line must pass straight through the next and previous boxes.
White Circle: Travel straight through the box, and the line must turn in the next and/or previous box.

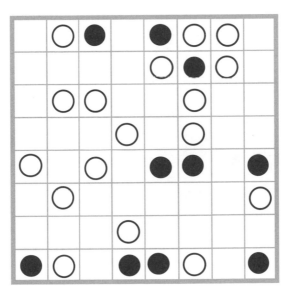

Answer on page 173

Roulette

The roulette ball is dropped into the wheel at the 0 section. When the ball falls into a number 15 seconds later, it has travelled at an average speed of 3 metres per second clockwise, while the wheel has travelled at an average 1 metre per second in the other direction. The ball starts rolling 50 centimetres away from the wheel's centre. Where does it land? Take pi as having a value of exactly 3.2.

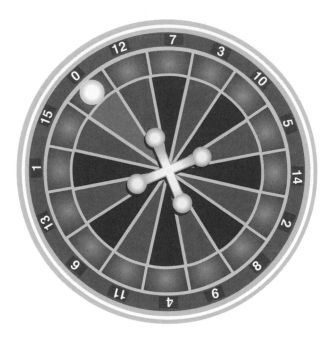

Answer on page 173

Scene It?

The four squares below can all be found in the picture grid – can you track them drown? Beware, they may not be the right way up!

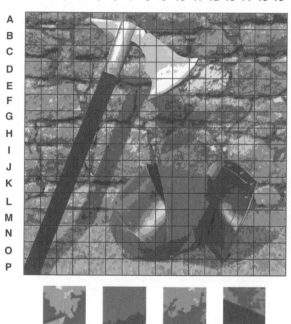

Answer on page 173

Sum People

Work out what number is represented by which person and replace the question mark.

25 30 ? 22

Shuffle

Fill up the shuffle box so that each row, column and long diagonal contains a Jack, Queen, King and Ace of each suit.

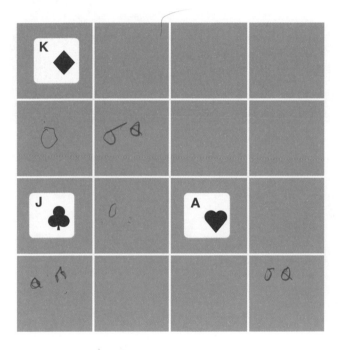

Answer on page 173

The Red Corner

Use the red corners to make the central number the same way in all three cases. What number should replace the question mark?

Answer on page 173

Riddle

At the rocket scientists' canteen, two boffins were chatting in the queue. "How many kids do you have?" asked Professor Numero. "Three" replied Doctor Egghead. "Oh yeah? How old?," said Professor Numero. "Ah," said Dr Egghead, "Well, their ages add up to 13 and multiply to 36, and two of them are twins". "Hmm…" said the Professor. "My eldest is a girl," said Dr Egghead. "Aha! That makes all the difference," said Professor Numero, and promptly told the good Doctor the ages of all his children.

How did that last piece of information help, and how old are the Doctor's kids?

9 2 2
1

Answer on page 173

Sum People

Work out which number is represented by which person and fill in the question mark.

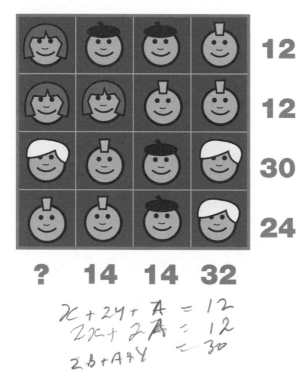

$$x + 2y + A = 12$$
$$2x + 2A = 12$$
$$2b + A + y = 30$$

Answer on page 174 ZA

Spare Part

All these pictures below show constructions built from three units of the spare part. Except one! Can you find the dodgy design?

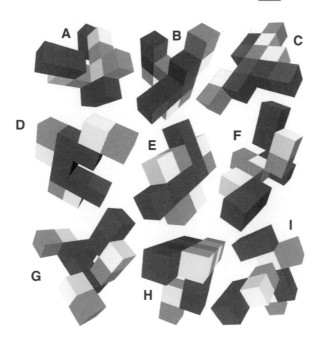

A

B

C

D

E

F

G

H

I

Answer on page 174

Minesweeper

The numbers in some squares in the grid indicate the exact number of black squares that should surround it. Shade these squares until all the numbers are surrounded by the correct number of black squares.

	2	1	1		3		2
4		3		1			
				1		1	1
4		4		2		0	
	2	2			3	3	
2		2	4				
	3					6	3
2			3	4		3	

Answer on page 174

More or Less

The arrows indicate whether a number in a box is greater or smaller than an adjacent number. Complete the grid so that all rows and columns contain the numbers 1 to 6.

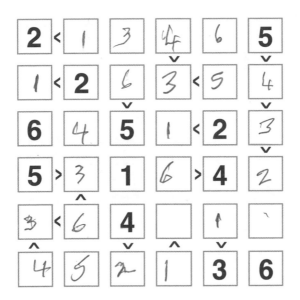

Answer on page 174

Next!

In the sequence below, which of the alternatives, A, B, C or D, should replace the question mark?

A **B** **C** **D**

  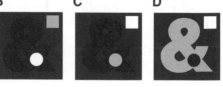

Answer on page 174

Patch of the Day

Place the patch over the grid so that no colour appears twice in the same row or column. Beware, the shape may not be the right way up!

Answer on page 174

Signpost

Can you crack the logical secret behind the numbers by these footballers' names, and work out what number Fabregas might be?

Ronaldinho
252

Rooney
162

Messi
91

Crespo
24

Fabregas
?

Answer on page 174

Shape Stacker

Can you work out the logic behind the numbers in these shapes, and the total of A + B?

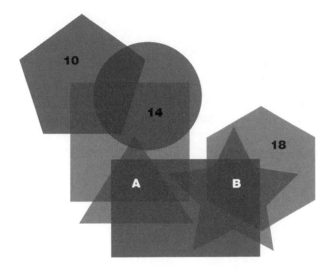

Answer on page 174

Scales

The arms of these scales are divided into sections — a weight two sections away from the middle will be twice as heavy as a weight one section away. Can you arrange the supplied weights in such a way as to balance the whole scale?

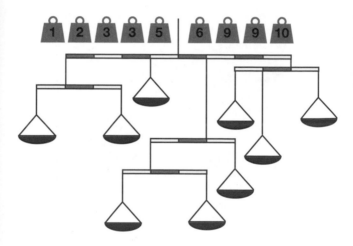

Answer on page 175

Safecracker

To open the safe, all the buttons must be pressed in the correct order before the "open" button is pressed. What is the first button pressed in your sequence?

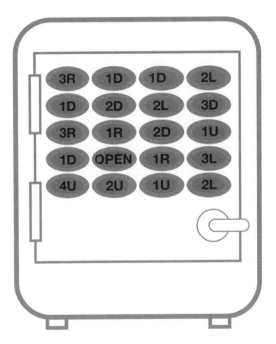

Answer on page 175

Radar

The numbers in some cells in the grid indicate the exact number of black cells that should border it. Shade these black, until all the numbers are surrounded by the correct number of black cells.

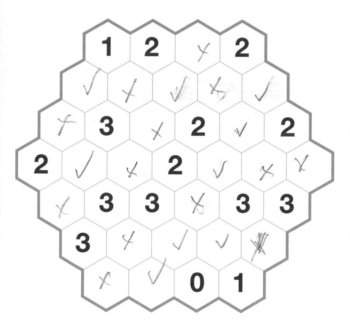

Answer on page 175

Pattern Pairs

Only one of the tiles below is unique; the other all have an exact matching pair. Can you find the one-off?

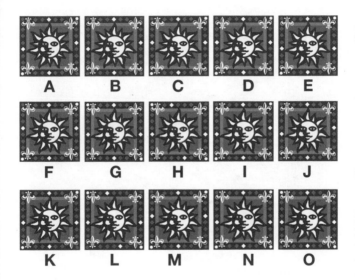

Answer on page 175

Odd One Out

Which of the shapes below is not the same as the other ones?

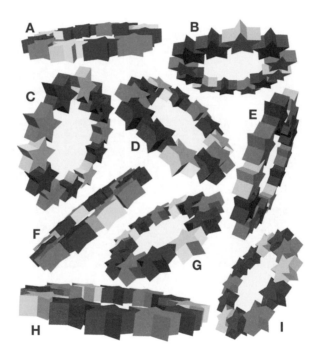

Answer on page 175

Plan View

Three of the patterns are a flat view of the picture below. Can you find the three that do not match?

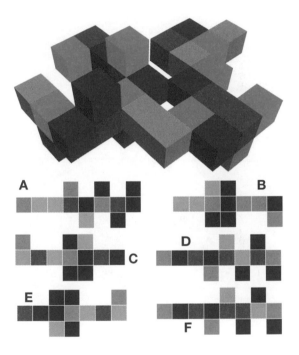

Answer on page 175

Where's the Pair?

Only two of the shapes below are exactly the same — can you find the matching pair?

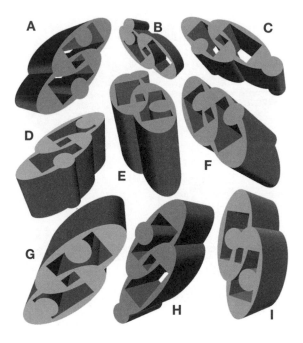

Answer on page 175

Answers

Page 6
Answer: B is the odd one out

Page 7
Answer: A

Page 8

0			1	2			2
1		2	1				2
		2		2	2	2	
2		2					0
	1	1	2		2	1	
2		1		2		2	1
	3			3	5		3
2		2	2				

Page 9

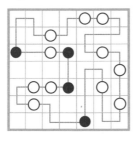

Page 10
Answer: B and G are the pair

Page 11
Answer: If its bordering cells are

predominantly blue, a cell becomes blue. If they are predominantly red, it becomes red. If the bordering cells are equal in number, the colour of a cell changes

Page 12

				▲			1
		▲	▲	▲			1
		▲		▲	▲	▲	2
▲	▲	▲					2
▲				▲	▲		2
▲	▲			▲			2
				▲			1
		▲	▲				1

2 0 4 0 0 4 0 1

Page 13

C	M	W	B	I	U
I	C	M	U	B	W
B	U	I	C	W	M
U	I	B	W	M	C
W	B	U	M	C	I
M	W	C	I	U	B

6	1	2	3	5	4
3	6	4	5	1	2
5	4	1	6	2	3
4	5	3	2	6	1
2	3	5	1	4	6
1	2	6	4	3	5

W + 2 = Y   M + 6 = S
I + 5 = N   C + 1 = D
U + 4 = Y   B + 3 = E

Answer: SYDNEY

Answers

Page 14

Answer: 6272 cubic centimetres. Each little cube measures 4 x 4 x 4 cm, or 64 cubic centimetres, and there are 98 little cubes left. 64 x 98 = 6272

Page 15

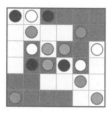

Page 16

Answer: B and F are the pair

Page 17

9	8	2	3	1	7	4	5	6
6	5	1	2	9	4	7	3	8
7	4	3	5	6	8	2	1	9
8	6	7	9	2	1	3	4	5
3	2	5	4	8	6	9	7	1
1	9	4	7	3	5	6	8	2
5	1	9	6	4	3	8	2	7
4	7	6	8	5	2	1	9	3
2	3	8	1	7	9	5	6	4

Page 18

Answer: L3, C13, O15, J5

Page 19

Answer:

1.   1
2.   1
3.   4
4.   3
5.   Red

Page 20

Answer: M

Page 21

Answer: There are 25 honeycomb cells and 8 bees. Multiply both figures by 4 and we get an occupation percentage of 32%. 6 out of 8 bees, or three-quarters, or 75%, are awake.

Answers

Page 22

Page 23

Page 24

Answer: 12. The inner numbers are made up of the two outer numbers of the opposite segment multiplied. 4 x 3 = 12

Page 25

Solution: If its bordering triangles are

predominantly black, a triangle becomes orange. If they are predominantly orange, it becomes black.

If the bordering cells are equal in number, the triangle becomes yellow, and if the bordering triangles have now become predominantly yellow, it also becomes yellow

Page 26

Answer:
Blue = Right
Red = Left
Green = Up
Yellow = Down
The final die in your trip is the red 3, top of the fourth column.

Page 27

Answer: Each pentagon contains numbers that add up to 20, with the sides nearest adjoining pentagons adding up to 10

Page 28

Page 29

5	1	4	6	2	3
6	4	5	3	1	2
4	2	3	1	6	5
3	6	2	4	5	1
2	3	1	5	4	6
1	5	6	2	3	4

Answers

Page 30

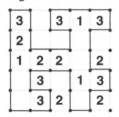

Page 31

Page 32

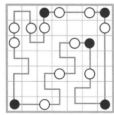

Page 33

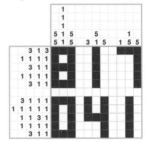

Page 34
Answer: E

Page 35

3	1	5	2	4
1	2	4	5	3
4	5	3	1	2
2	3	1	4	5
5	4	2	3	1

Page 36
Answer: E is the odd one out

Page 37
Answer: E

Answers

Page 38
Answer: B, C & D are not views

Page 39
Answer: C10, J4, M11, H7

Page 40
Answer: 2520
The numbers represent the number of sides in the shape they occupy. When shapes overlap, the numbers are added together.

A: $6 + 4 + 4 = 14$
B: $10 + 4 + 4 = 18$
C: $5 + 4 + 1 = 10$

$14 \times 18 \times 10 = 2520$

Page 41
Answer: D

Page 42

7	1	9	8	6	3	5	2	4
2	3	6	1	5	4	7	9	8
8	5	4	2	9	7	1	3	6
1	6	2	7	8	5	9	4	3
3	4	5	9	1	2	6	8	7
9	7	8	3	4	6	2	1	5
4	2	1	6	7	8	3	5	9
5	9	7	4	3	1	8	6	2
6	8	3	5	2	9	4	7	1

Page 43
Answer: 25

 4

 5

 6

 9

Page 44
Answer: 55

 1

 5

 10

 20

Page 45
Answer: Purple = 2, Red = 3, Yellow = 4, Green = 5, Blue = 6. Four green balls are required

Answers

Page 46
Answer: C and H are the pair

Page 47
Answer: A

Page 48
Answer: B4, M7, F12, P11

Page 49
Answer: G

Page 50
Answer: C

Page 51

Page 52
Answer:
Blue = Right
Red = Left
Green = Up
Yellow = Down
The final die in your trip is the yellow 6, top of the third column

Page 53
Answer: D. The number six is turned 90 degrees compared to the other dice

Page 54

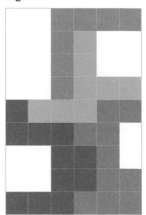

Answers

Page 55
Answer: 6. Subtract the total of the pink circle numbers from the total of the yellow circle numbers in both cases

Page 56
Answer: A, C, E and F

Page 57

B	F	E	A	C	D
F	A	D	C	E	B
D	C	A	B	F	E
A	E	C	D	B	F
C	B	F	E	D	A
E	D	B	F	A	C

Page 58

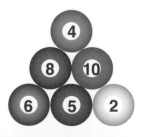

Page 59

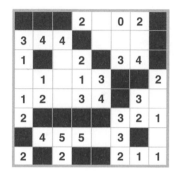

Page 60
Answer: J

Page 61
Answer: 720
Blue shapes have a value equal to the number of sides they have. Green shapes have a value of
2 x the number of sides they have. Where shapes overlap, their totals are multiplied.

(A) 8 x 8 x 10 = 640 +
(B) 10 x 8 x 1 = 80. Total 720

Answers

Page 62
Answer: D

Page 63

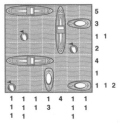

				5
				3
				1 1
				2
				4
				1
				1 1 2

1 1 1 1 4 1 1
1 1 1 3   1 1
1 1   1

Page 64

				▲	▲		2
▲							0
	▲		▲		▲	▲	4
			▲				0
							0
				▲	▲	▲	2
▲					▲		1
▲					▲	▲	1

1 2 0 1 1 1 3 1

Page 65

Page 66

3	1	2	2		3
3		2		2	2
2	2		2		
	3	1	3	3	2
2		2		2	
2	2		2		2

Page 67

1	5	2 < 3	6 > 4
2	6	3	4 < 5	1
6	4	5	1	2 < 3
5 > 3	1	2	4	6
3	2	4 < 6	1	5
4	1	6 > 5	3	2

Page 68

8	2	1	2	2	4
6	3	1	1	6	3
4	9	9	9	3	5
5	7	1	5	5	5
2	7	3	1	6	4
9	7	3	2	3	7

Page 69

1D	1R	2D	3L
1R	3D	1R	1U
OPEN	2U	1U	2D
1D	2R	2L	1U
2U	1U	1U	1L

164

Answers

Page 70

5	2	9	1	6	8	3	4	7
1	3	7	9	2	4	6	8	5
4	6	8	7	3	5	1	9	2
6	7	1	4	5	9	2	3	8
3	9	4	2	8	1	5	7	6
2	8	5	6	7	3	4	1	9
7	1	6	8	4	2	9	5	3
8	4	3	5	9	6	7	2	1
9	5	2	3	1	7	8	6	4

Page 71

Answer: green 1, pink 2, purple 3, red 4

Page 72

Answer: D and I are the pair

Page 73

Answer: If its bordering squares (not diagonals) are predominantly red, a square becomes red. If they are predominantly blue it becomes blue. If the bordering cell colours are equal in number, the square becomes grey and if the bordering squares have now become predominantly grey, a square also becomes grey

Page 74

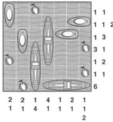

Page 75

Page 76

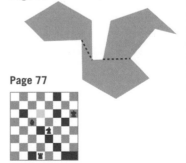

Page 77

Answers

Answer: Each pentagon contains numbers that add up to 24, with the sides facing each other on adjoining pentagons, when multiplied together, also making 24

Page 79

Answer: A. Each row and column in the grid contains shapes whose sides total 12, two of which are yellow and one of which is red

Page 80

3	1	4	5	2	6
5	6	1	2	3	4
1	5	6	3	4	2
2	4	3	1	6	5
4	3	2	6	5	1
6	2	5	4	1	3

Page 81

Answer: 2 . Divide the total of the numbers in the blue circles by the total of the numbers in the green circles in each case

Page 82

1		2		2	2	
2	2	3	2			3
	0	3	2	2	2	
	3			2		
1		2	2	1	2	
3	2	2	2			3

Page 83

5	10	9
12	8	4
7	6	11

Page 84

Page 85

Answer: There are 38 red squares in the design, which is made up of 100 squares, so 38% of the design is red. There are 24 blue squares, 6 of which have stars on them, so one quarter, or 25% of the blue squares contain stars

Answers

Page 86

Answer: J12, B2, P9, F7

Page 87

	Forest	Roadside	Field	Jar	Bottle	Matchbox	Morning	Afternoon	Evening
Beetle	◯	◯	◯	✕	◯	✕	◯	✕	◯
Spider	◯	✕	◯	✕	◯	◯	◯	◯	✕
Butterfly	✕	◯	◯	◯	◯	✕	✕	◯	◯
Morning	◯	◯	✕	◯	✕	◯			
Afternoon	✕	◯	◯	◯	◯	✕			
Evening	◯	✕	◯	✕	◯	◯			
Jar	◯	✕	◯						
Bottle	◯	◯	✕						
Matchbox	✕	◯	◯						

Page 88

1	2	6	9	7	8	5	3	4
8	4	7	1	3	5	2	9	6
3	5	9	6	4	2	1	7	8
9	6	1	8	5	3	7	4	2
7	3	4	2	1	6	9	8	5
2	8	5	7	9	4	6	1	3
4	1	2	3	6	7	8	5	9
6	7	3	5	8	9	4	2	1
5	9	8	4	2	1	3	6	7

Page 89

Answer:

1. 2
2. 2
3. Pink
4. E
5. 2

Page 90

2	8	9	6	4	7	3	1	5
4	5	7	1	8	3	6	2	9
6	3	1	9	5	2	7	8	4
1	9	4	2	3	8	5	6	7
8	7	2	5	9	6	4	3	1
5	6	3	7	1	4	8	9	2
9	1	8	3	7	5	2	4	6
3	2	4	4	6	1	9	7	8
7	4	6	8	2	9	1	5	3

Page 91

Answer: 36. Add all the red corners and multiply the total by two. $3 + 3 + 7 + 5 = 18 \times 2 = 36$

Page 92

[chessboard puzzle image]

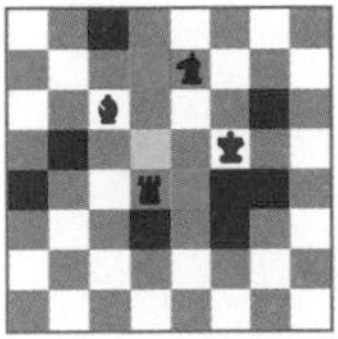

Page 93

B+6=H Z+1=A K+3=N Y+5=D A+4=E J+2=L

Solution: HANDEL

Z	K	A	B	Y	J
B	A	Y	J	Z	K
K	Y	B	A	J	Z
Y	J	Z	K	B	A
A	B	J	Z	K	Y
J	Z	K	Y	A	B

2	1	6	4	3	5
1	4	3	2	5	6
3	5	4	6	1	2
4	2	1	5	6	3
5	6	2	1	3	4
6	3	5	4	1	2

Answers

Page 94

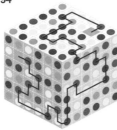

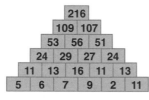

= up

= left

= down

= right

Page 95
Answer: N

Page 96
Answer: A, E & F are not views

Page 97

		216			
	109	107			
	53	56	51		
	24	29	27	24	
	11	13	16	11	13
5	6	7	9	2	11

Page 98

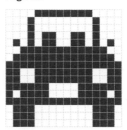

Page 99
Answer: O2, C15, H14, E6

Page 100
Answer: 2484 cubic centimetres. Each little cube measures
3 x 3 x 3 cm, or 27 cubic centimetres, and there are 92 little cubes left. 27 x 92 = 2484

Page 101
Answer: B. The right hand side should be showing a six

Answers

Page 102

Page 103

5	1	6	4	2	3
4	3	1	5	6	2
6	2	5	1	3	4
3	6	4	2	1	5
1	5	2	3	4	6
2	4	3	6	5	1

Page 104

Page 105

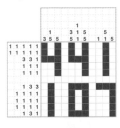

Page 106

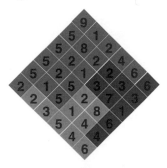

Page 107

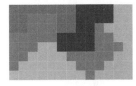

Page 108

Answer: Facing left with a pink tail. Two pigs with the same coloured tail are followed by a left-facing pig. Two pigs facing the same way are followed by one with a pink tail

Page 109

Answer: A, C, E and H

Answers

Page 110

Page 111

Page 112

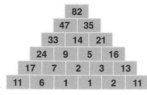

Page 113

Page 114
Answer: Purple = 3, Green = 4, Blue = 5, Yellow = 6, Red = 7. Three red balls are required

Page 115
Answer: D

Page 116
Answer: H

Page 117
Answer:
Orange 1
Black 2
Blue 3
Green 4

Answers

Page 118

2	3	2	1	3	2
3	0	3	1	2	2
2	2	2	1	1	2
2	2	3	3	3	2
3	0	2	0	2	2
2	3	3	3	2	1

Page 119

9	8	1	2	3	7	5	6	4
3	7	5	4	6	1	2	9	8
2	4	6	9	8	5	7	3	1
8	6	7	1	2	9	3	4	5
1	9	4	3	5	6	8	2	7
5	3	2	7	4	8	9	1	6
6	1	3	5	7	2	4	8	9
7	2	8	6	9	4	1	5	3
4	5	9	8	1	3	6	7	2

Page 120

 Every vertical and horizontal line contains one purple, one yellow and one white outer box. Each line also contains one purple inner diamond and two yellow ones. Finally each line contains one purple star and two yellow ones. The missing image should be a yellow outer box with a purple inner diamond and a yellow star

Page 121

Answer: B and G are the pair

Page 122

Answer: C. Each row and column in the grid contains a target, two gold arrows (one pointing left and one right) and three blue arrows (two of which point right and one left)

Page 123

Answer: 6. There were 12 prisoners in the hold before the escape, making 40 people in all on the ship, and 15 percent of 40 is 6

Page 124

2	9	3	5	1	8	4	6	7
8	4	5	3	6	7	2	9	1
1	7	6	9	4	2	3	5	8
4	6	2	7	8	9	1	3	5
3	1	9	2	5	6	8	7	4
5	8	7	4	3	1	6	2	9
6	3	1	8	7	5	9	4	2
9	5	4	1	2	3	7	8	6
7	2	8	6	9	4	5	1	3

Page 125

Answer:
1. Blue
2. Blue
3. 4
4. 7
5. 4

Answers

Page 126

Answer: 4. Multiply all the numbers in pink circles and add all the numbers in green circles. Divide the pink total by the green one.

$3 \times 2 \times 4 \times 2 = 48$

$1 + 6 + 2 + 3 = 12$

48 divided by 12 is 4

Page 127

	Monday	Tuesday	Wednesday	Mercedes	Ferrari	Porsche	Silver	Black	Gold
Tyres	X	◯	◯	X	◯	◯	X	◯	◯
Oil	◯	X	◯	◯	X	◯	◯	◯	X
Lights	◯	◯	X	◯	◯	X	◯	X	◯
Silver	X	◯	◯	X	◯	◯			
Black	◯	◯	X	◯	X	◯			
Gold	◯	X	◯	◯	◯	X			
Mercedes	X	◯	◯						
Ferrari	◯	X	◯						
Porsche	◯	◯	X						

Page 128

Answer: 2,900 square millimetres. Each 20 x 20 square represents 400 mm². 5 squares, 4 half-square triangles and 2 half-squares make up the tree (3,200). Minus 300mm² that make up the oranges

Page 129

Page 130

B	F	C	D	A	E
D	A	F	B	E	C
E	C	A	F	B	D
A	E	B	C	D	F
F	D	E	A	C	B
C	B	D	E	F	A

Page 131

Answer: There are 135 squares in the design. 50 are white and 4 contain stars. 135 divided by 54 is 2.5. 100 divided by 2.5 is 40, so 54 represents 40% of 135. The squares that are not white and do not contain stars must therefore represent the other 60%

Page 132

10	9	14
15	11	7
8	13	12

Page 133

Answer: 22 and a half revolutions of cog A, which will make exactly 20 revolutions of cog B, 18 revolutions of cog C and 10 revolutions of cog D

Answers

Page 134

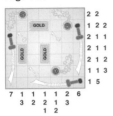

```
        2 2
        1 2 2
        2 1 1
        2 1 1
        2 1 2
        1 1 3
        1 5
7 1 1 1 1 2 6
  3 2 2 1 3
      1 2
```

Page 135

Page 136

Answer: In the number 6 space. The ball travels at a speed of 4 metres per second (relative to the wheel) for 15 seconds, making a distance of 6000 centimetres in a clockwise direction. The circumference of the wheel is 320 centimetres (2 x pi (3.2) x radius (50cm)). The ball must then travel 18.75 laps of the wheel, placing it three quarters of the way around the wheel in a clockwise direction, in the 6 space

Page 137
Answer: F8, N10, B16, O2

Page 138
Answer: 27

 2

 4

 6

 13

Page 139

Page 140

Answer: 50. Multiply the two largest red corners, then multiply the two smallest corners. Subtract the smaller total from the larger. 8 x 7 = 56. 6 x 1 = 6. 56 − 6 = 50

Page 141

Answer: 9, 2 and 2. Before he knew that the twins were younger than the single child, the Professor could have come up with the answer 6, 6 and 1

Answers

Page 142
Answer: 18

 3

 1

 5

 11

Page 143
Answer: B

Page 144

	2	1	1		3		2
4		3		1			
				1		1	1
4		4		2		0	
	2	2			3	3	
2		2	4				
	3					6	3
2			3	4		3	

Page 145

2	‹	6	3	4	1	5
1	‹	2	6	3	5	4
6	4	5	1	2	3	
5	3	1	6	4	2	
3	5	4	2	6	1	
4	1	2	5	3	6	

Page 146
Answer: C. With each new image,
the dot takes the colour of the previous
box, the square takes the colour of the
previous dot, the ampersand takes the
colour of the previous square, and the
box takes the colour of the previous
ampersand

Page 147

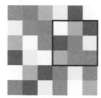

Page 148
Answer: 66. Score one for a consonant and
two for a vowel, then multiply the total by
the alphabetical position of the first letter.
$5 + 6 = 11$, $11 \times 6 = 66$

Page 149
Answer: 85. Pink shapes have
a value equal to twice the number of sides
they have. Blue shapes have a value of 3
x the number of sides they have. Where
shapes overlap, their totals are added
together. (A) $8 + 9 + 12 = 29 +$
(B) $8 + 18 + 30 = 56$. Total 85

Answers

Page 150

Page 152

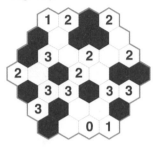

Page 151

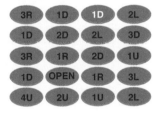

Page 153
Answer: N

Page 154
Answer: F is the odd one out

Page 155
Answer: B, C and F are not views

Page 156
Answer: C and H are the pair

Your puzzle notes